MILITARY VETERANS, POST-TRAUMATIC STRESS DISORDER, AND THE DEATH PENALTY

This publication is designed to provide accurate and authoritative information in regard to the subject matter covered. It is sold with the understanding that neither the author, nor the publisher, is engaged in rendering legal, psychological, or any other professional services. If legal advice or other expert assistance is required, the services of a competent professional person should be sought.

The author acknowledges the information contained within this publication is self-purported by personal experiences and vast military training. The author served sixteen years on active duty with the United States military in the Department of the Air Force. The positions and opinions stated herein are those of the author alone and do not represent the views of the U.S. Government, the Department of Defense, the Department of the Air Force, or any other governmental or non-governmental agency. It is also the authors understanding of legal cases.

- *From a Declaration of Principles Jointly Adopted by a Committee of the American Bar Association and a Committee of Publishers and Associations.*

To the men and women of the United States Armed Forces past, present,

and future, the law enforcement professionals, and all others who suffer

from Post-Traumatic Stress Disorder.

\-   Jason Boswell

Contents

PREFACE

This book examines the lives of United States service members and veterans who have combat-related Post-Traumatic Stress Disorder (PTSD), have been convicted of a capital offense, and subsequently, have been sentenced to death. It will also present the reader with clear and convincing evidence to demonstrate why service members and veterans with combat-related PTSD should not receive this penalty and why it should be considered cruel and unusual punishment. The United States Supreme Court has previously ruled that the execution of mentally disabled individuals fall within this perimeter, and so should service members and veterans with Post-Traumatic Stress Disorder, due to their diminished culpability. This book also introduces the idea of establishing and classifying a categorical exclusion for past and present military members who may be considered high-risk due to their combat experience.

ACKNOWLEDGMENTS

This book is the product of several years of dedicated research, analysis, and hard work. The information contained herein was collected and published while working on my Master of Arts degree in Legal Studies. While completing the degree requirements one class at a time, I realized that at the same time, numerous military members were returning from overseas deployments and experiencing PTSD related issues and dealing with the law. The material may be outdated in the readers view, but the overall data, evidence, and information is still valid.

Through personal experience and great friendships, I have had the opportunity to gain insight and knowledge concerning this debilitating disorder through the courage and sacrifice of the men and women of the U.S. Armed

Forces, law enforcement professionals, and other individuals. Although some may not agree with all I have to say in this book, I have drawn on their attitudes, experiences, and desire to move forward with their lives.

I am, and always will be, in their debt.

The Problem

Over the last fifty years, the United States has devoted all branches of the military to combat service in numerous operations around the globe. Today's veterans consist of members who have served in conflicts or warzones to include the Vietnam War, Operation Urgent Fury in Grenada, Operation El Dorado Canyon in Libya, Operation Just Cause in Panama, Operation Desert Storm in the Gulf, as well as Operations Enduring Freedom and Iraqi Freedom in Afghanistan and Iraq.[1] Additionally, veterans have also played a part in non-combat situations such as Somalia and Kosovo.[2]

---

[1] THE OFFICE OF GENERAL COUNSEL, U.S. SENTENCING COMMISSION REPORT, 2 (Jan. 2012).

[2] THE OFFICE OF GENERAL COUNSEL, *supra* note 1, at 2.

Of the approximately 1.5 million troops[3] expected to be

discharged from the Armed Forces after returning to the

U.S. from serving in Iraq and Afghanistan, up to twenty

percent[4] could very well become afflicted with Post-

Traumatic Stress Disorder (PTSD). If history repeats itself,

the number of soldiers who could suffer from this disease

has the potential to rise, as did the number of veterans who

served in the Vietnam conflict. It has been estimated that

almost seventy percent of the troops who returned from

Vietnam suffered from PTSD. [5]

To put this into numbers that could affect the criminal

justice system, straightforward math reveals that this would

introduce an additional 375,000 cases, all of which could

---

[3] VETERANS DISABILITY BENEFITS COMMISSION, HONORING THE CALL TO DUTY: VETERANS DISABILITY BENEFITS IN THE 21ST CENTURY, 383 (Oct. 2007)

[4] U.S. DEPT OF VETERAN AFFAIRS, NATIONAL CENTER FOR PTSD, FACT SHEET, HOW COMMON IS PTSD? available at http://ncptsd.va.gov/ncmain/ncdocs/factshts/fshowcommon/isptsd.html (last visited August 21, 2012).

[5] Davidson, Michael J., *Post-Traumatic Stress Disorder: A Controversy Defense for Veterans of a Conversational War,* 29 WM & MARY L. REV. 415 (1988).

utilize a defense of PTSD.[6] Of these individuals, most of
may not receive the appropriate punishment or sentence for
the crime. Many military men and women who have served
in war zones, some of whom have served multiple tours,
return to the United States suffering from this debilitating
disorder. Many of those suffering from the disease commit
criminal offenses, and some of those individuals commit
capital offenses and face the ultimate punishment. This book
attempts to make the argument that military members and
veterans who have PTSD should not receive the death
penalty. Such a sentence should be considered cruel and
unusual punishment.

---

[6] Erin M. Grover, *Iraq as a Psychological Quagmire: The Implications
of Using Post-Traumatic Stress Disorder as a Defense for Iraq War
Veterans*, 28 PACE L. REV. 561 (2008).

CHAPTER 2

Defining the Purpose

The overall purpose of this book is to show that the death penalty should be considered cruel and unusual if a military member or veteran is sentenced to death upon conviction of a capital offense, either after returning from or while in a war zone and has been clinically diagnosed with Post-Traumatic Stress Disorder. As you continue to read this book, you will first find the definition as well as the symptoms and consequences of PTSD and the death penalty. Second, I will provide a brief history of PTSD as well as other mental illnesses and the death penalty. Third, I will examine and review criminal cases ranging from 1972 to the present, in which PTSD and the death penalty were examined. Fourth, this study will show a need for significant changes within the eyes of the courts when a military member or veteran, who suffers from combat related PTSD commits a capital offense and faces the death penalty. Lastly, this study will introduce a viable alternative to this punishment and show why this sentence should be considered cruel and unusual.

By 2014, over 1.5 million military members of the United States Armed Forces will have served in or around various theatres of active combat.[7] As more and more service members continue to serve in combat zones and in more than one deployment, it has been estimated that as many as one in five of these members who return stateside will have suffered from either Traumatic Brain Injury or Post-Traumatic Stress Disorder during their deployment period.[8] Moreover, researchers have found that that over twenty-five percent of the service members who participated in and survived heavy combat in Vietnam have since been charged with a criminal offense.[9] This is a statistic that we as a nation, cannot afford, with service members returning from Afghanistan and Iraq.

---

[7] VETERANS DISABILITY BENEFITS COMMISSION, *supra* note 3, at 383.

[8] Davidson, *supra* note 5, at 415.

[9] Ann R. Auberry, *PTSD: Effective Representation of a Vietnam Veteran in the Criminal Justice System,* 68 MARQ. L. REV. 647, 650 (1985).

As some military members transition back into a way of life in the United States after serving numerous and lengthy deployments in war zones, it has become apparent that PTSD is a viable defense in an attempt to avoid the ultimate penalty - death. From isolated incidents ranging from domestic violence that ends in another's death, to a shooting spree in two Afghan villages, some military members are on trial and claiming to suffer from this disorder. With the judicial system having little insight and history into this new epidemic, this study will attempt to show that the death penalty should be considered cruel and unusual if the accused service member suffers from combat related PTSD during the commission of a capital offense.

The concept behind this theory will show that the death penalty should be considered cruel and unusual if a service member or veteran, who suffers from combat related PTSD, receives this sentence after committing a capital offense.

In order to prove this theory, this book will examine 1) the history of PTSD; 2) the definition, symptoms and consequences of PTSD; 3) mental illnesses and the death penalty; 4) criminal cases in which PTSD and the death penalty were examined; 5) the significance of PTSD in capital cases and how the court's view service members and veteran defendants; and finally, 6) the significance for a categorical exclusion and how the courts can apply its own judgment to this dilemma.

CHAPTER **3**

Significance of PTSD Research

There seems to be very little information regarding military-related PTSD and capital punishment. Nonetheless, some definable trends are beginning to emerge as this disorder continues to be used as a defense in courtrooms throughout the nation. Although there are limited cases involving service members returning from combat theaters who suffer from PTSD, a number of these members have committed capital offenses while claiming they suffer from this disorder. Some of these cases have yet to reach the courtroom which may provide future guidance and more importantly, case law.

PTSD will undoubtedly not only affect the civilian residences and communities of all countries, but the criminal justice and court system will feel the influence of this dilemma as well.

PTSD will undoubtedly not only affect the civilian residences and communities of all countries, but the criminal justice and court system will feel the influence of this dilemma as well. This thesis will examine the emerging trend of service members and veterans with PTSD and why imposing the death penalty on these individuals suffering from PTSD should be considered cruel and unusual punishment.

This book will show the existing policies within the state of legal knowledge, as well as show how the higher courts have ruled when dealing with individuals who commit a capital offense and are mentally impaired during the commission of the crime. The book will also examine whether the death penalty should apply in these types of legal cases and why the U.S. Supreme Court should rule that it cannot apply the death penalty under the cruel and unusual punishment clause.

CHAPTER 4

History of PTSD

In the early 1800's, military doctors started to diagnose soldiers with "exhaustion" following the stressors found in war-zones.[10] This "exhaustion" was illustrated by the soldiers' mental shutdown due to their individual or even group trauma.[11] Similarly, todays soldiers are expected not to be afraid or show any fear before, during or after battle.

During the early 1800's, the only real treatment for exhaustion was to relieve the solider of duty and allow them to decompress for a short period of time.[12] After their decompression period was over, the solider was then placed back into battle. Throughout this process and oftentimes during extreme and repeated stress, these service members became extremely fatigued as a part of the human body's

---

[10] I.S. Parrish, Military Veterans PTSD Reference Manual, 2, (2001), available at http://www.ptsd manual.com/chap1.htm (last visited Sept. 19, 2012).

[11] Id. at 1.

[12] Id. at 1.

natural shock reaction.[13]

During the same time period, England created a syndrome known as "railway spine" or "railway hysteria" that displayed an incredible likeness to what we call PTSD today.[14] This syndrome was exhibited by individuals who had been in the tragic railway accidents of that time period.[15] In 1876, Dr. Mendez DaCosta published a paper diagnosing Civil War combat veterans with "Soldiers Heart" in which he stated that the symptoms of this syndrome included startle responses, hyper-vigilance, and heart arrhythmia.[16] The known term "shell shock" materialized during World War I and was followed in World War II by the term known as "combat fatigue."[17]

---

[13] Id. at 1.

[14] *Id.* at 2.

[15] *Id.*

[16] *Id.*

[17] *Id.*

These terms were used to describe military veterans who displayed large amounts of stress and anxiety as the result of combat trauma.[18] The official designation of "Post Traumatic Stress Disorder" did not emerge until 1980, when the Third edition of the Diagnostic and Statistical Manual of Mental Disorders (DSM) was published.[19]

PTSD has spawned several similar legal defenses known as the "Holocaust Syndrome"; "Battered Child Syndrome"; "The Battle Fatigue Syndrome"; and "The Love Fear Syndrome."[20]

The Diagnostic and Statistical Manual of Mental Disorders (DSM) is known as the "bible" of mental illnesses and was initially published by the American Psychiatric Association(APA).[21]

---

[18] *Id.*

[19] *Id.*

[20] Ralph Slovenko, *The Watering Down of PTSD in Criminal Law,* J. OF PSYCHIATRY & L., 421, (2004).

[21] *Id.* at 421.

This manual provides the clinical and approved definition of all mental illnesses. When this Manual was first published in 1952, what we now classify as PTSD was then classified as "stress response syndrome" and was thought to be caused by "gross stress reaction."[22]

In the second edition (DSM-II), which was published in 1968, the trauma-related disorders were grouped together and labelled "situational disorders."[23] Vietnam Veterans who were treated for this situational disorder were advised that if their symptoms lasted more than six months after their return from the warzone, that they had a "pre-existing" condition which made it a "transient situational disorder," and that the problem was in no way service related.[24]

This knowledge resulted in a large number of veterans "walking wounded" and if researched further, could be

---

[22] Parrish, *supra* note 10, at 2.

[23] *Id.*

[24] *Id.*

attributed to the high suicide rate suffered by Vietnam Veterans at that time.[25]

Finally, in the DSM-III, the title "Post-traumatic Stress Disorder" was utilized and placed under the sub-category of "anxiety disorders." In the current edition DSM-IV, Post-Traumatic Stress Disorder is again applied; however, it has now been repositioned under the new "stress response" category and continues to remain in the "anxiety disorder" category.[26]

As shown, what was initially defined as a syndrome eventually transformed into a disorder. According to Taber's Cyclopedic Medical Dictionary, a syndrome is "a group of signs and symptoms that collectively characterize or indicate a particular disease or abnormal condition" and

---

[25] Patience H.C. Mason, *Recovering from the War: A Woman's Guide to Helping Your Vietnam Vet, Your Family, and Yourself,* 98 (1990).

[26] Parrish, *supra* note 10, at 2.

a disorder is "an illness."[27]

With this newly classified disorder, PTSD has since changed from being part of a collective indicator into a singular illness which is a substantial medical distinction.[28] The legal significance of a disorder is of important distinction as cited in *Vergara v. Lopez-Vasquez,* 510 N.W. 2d 550 (1993), where Justice Wright of the Court of Appeals of Nebraska ruled that "[A] person with a mental disorder is one who suffers from a condition of mental derangement which actually prevents the sufferer from understanding his or her legal rights or from instituting legal action."

---

[27] Donald Venus, *Taber's Cyclopedic Medical Dictionary*, 1006 (21st ed. 2009).

[28] *Id.* at 1007.

CHAPTER **5**

Post-Traumatic Stress Disorder

PTSD can develop after a military member (or any human being) experiences a life-threatening or highly traumatic event, such as military combat, rape, abuse (sexual or physical), or terrorist attacks.[29] In order to understand what happens within the human body when an individual experiences such an event, it will be explained in simple terms. During, or even after an event, the body produces an involuntary physiological stress response. This begins in the reticular activating system and continues to the hypothalamus.[30]

---

[29] U.S. DEP'T OF VETERAN AFFAIRS, NATIONAL CENTER FOR PTSD, WHAT IS PTSD?, available at http://www.ncptsd.va.gov/ncmain/ncdocs/fact-shts/fs-what-is-ptsd.html (last visited Sept. 21, 2012).

[30] Edgar Garcia-Rill & Erica Beecher-Monas, *Gatekeeping Stress: The Science and Admissibility of Post-Traumatic Stress Disorder*, 24 U. ARK. LITTLE ROCK, Rev. 9 (2001).

The hypothalamus signals the pituitary gland to secrete a hormone known as the adrenocorticotropic hormone or ACTH, which ultimately causes the body to produce adrenaline.[31] The adrenaline then causes a palpable stress, which includes a rapid heartbeat, pain desensitizing and hyper-alertness. Finally, the brain terminates this stress response when needed in what is known as a negative feedback process, where additional ACTH is released in order to terminate the ongoing production of ACTH.[32] Military members who suffer from PTSD experience this stress response whenever there is a reminder of the event(s) that caused the onset of this disorder, such as a mental flashback, a triggering image(s) or sounds, or even a closely related incident. The individual is consequently under continuous stress, which may have a "deleterious effect on the brain."[33]

---

[31] Edgar Garcia-Rill & Erica Beecher-Monas, *Gatekeeping Stress: The Science and Admissibility of Post-Traumatic Stress Disorder, UALR L. Rev* 24 (2001): 9.

[32] *Id.*

[33] *Id.*

The National Institute of Mental Health defines PTSD as "an anxiety disorder"[34] that some people develop after seeing or living through a dangerous event. This fear can trigger many split-second changes in the human body in an attempt to prepare to defend itself against the perceived danger or to simply avoid it. This "fight or flight" response is a healthy reaction aimed at protecting a person from harm.[35] In PTSD, this fight or flight reaction can become changed or even damaged. People who suffer from PTSD may feel a sense of stress or become frightened even when they are no longer in danger.[36]

Surveys of service personnel reveal some of the circumstances that contribute to the development of PTSD. These include: "being attacked or ambushed, . .

---

[34] NATIONAL INSTITUTE OF MENTAL HEALTH, WHAT IS POST-TRAUMATIC STRESS DISORDER, OR PTSD?, available at http://www.nimh.nih.gov/health/publications/post-traumatic-stress-disorder-ptsd/what-is-post-traumatic-stress-disorder-or-ptsd.shtml (last viewed Aug. 21, 2012).

[35] *Id.*

[36] *Id.*

being shot at or receiving small arms fire, . . . seeing dead bodies or human remains, . . . knowing someone else seriously injured or killed, . . . seeing ill or injured women or children whom they were unable to help, . . . [having] a buddy shot or hit who was near them, . . . and engaging in hand-to-hand combat."[37]

---

[37] Don Nidiffer and Spencer Leach, *To Hell and Back: Evolution of Combat-Related Stress Disorder*, 29 DEV. MENTAL HEALTH L. 1, 11-12 (January, 2010) (citing Hoge, et al, *Combat Duty in Iraq and Afghanistan, Mental Health Problems, and Barriers to Care*, NEW ENG. J. OF MED., 351, 13-22 (2004)).

CHAPTER 6

Clinical Definition of Post-Traumatic Stress Disorder

The initial definition of PTSD was described as a psychological condition which was experienced by a person who had faced a traumatic event. This would have been caused by a catastrophic stressor outside the range of usual human experience such as war, torture, rape, or natural disaster.[38] This definition separated PTSD stressors from the "ordinary stressors" that were characterized in the DSM-III as "Adjustment Disorders," such as divorce, failure, rejection and financial problems.[39]

In 2000, the American Psychiatric Association (APA) revised the PTSD diagnostic criteria in the Fourth Edition of its Diagnostic and Statistical Manual of Mental Disorders (DSM-IV-TR) which defines Post-Traumatic

---

[38] Parrish, *supra* note 10, at 3.

[39] *Id.*

Stress Disorder as occurring when:

A. The person has been exposed to a traumatic event in which both of the following are present: [40]

(1) "The person has experienced, witnessed, or been confronted with an event or events that involve actual or threatened death or serious injury, or a threat to the physical integrity of oneself or others."[41] This could be the result of combat, friendly fire, being mortared or rocketed, wounded, captured or being taken hostage.[42]

(2) "The person's response involved intense fear, helplessness, or horror." [43] This may be seen through the soldier having a friend who was wounded or in the loss or attack of other squad members or seeing anyone who has recently died or injured.

---

[40] AMERICAN PSYCHIATRIC ASSOCIATION, DIAGNOSTIC AND STATISTICAL MANUAL OF MENTAL DISORDERS, 467 (4th ed. 2000).

[41] *Id.*

[42] *Id.*

[43] *Id.*

According to the DSM-IV,

B. The traumatic event is persistently re-experienced in one (or more) of the following ways: [44]

(1) "recurrent and intrusive distressing recollections of the event, including images, thoughts, or perceptions."[45]

(2) "recurrent distressing dreams of the event."[46]

(3) "acting or feeling as if the traumatic event were recurring"[47] which can include a sense of reliving the experience, illusions, hallucinations, and dissociative flashback episodes.

(4) "intense psychological distress at exposure to internal or external cues that symbolize or resemble an aspect of the traumatic event",

---

[44] *Id* at 468.

[45] *Id.*

[46] *Id.*

[47] *Id.*

(5) "physiological reactivity on exposure to internal or external cues that symbolize or resemble an aspect of the traumatic event."

C. "Persistent avoidance of stimuli associated with the trauma and numbing of general responsiveness (not present before the trauma), as indicated by at least three (or more) of the following:"[48]

(1) "efforts to avoid thoughts, feelings or conversations associated with the trauma." This can be seen through one trying not to think about combat or never wanting to be happy due to a battle that ensued when that individual was feeling good earlier in the day or trying never to get angry because they are afraid of what they might do or how they might react.

(2) "efforts to avoid activities, places, or people that arouse recollections of the trauma" such as not watching action or violent movies as before, not

---

[48] *Id.*

participating in ceremonies or activities like veteran's day parades or associate with other veterans.

(3) "the inability to recall an important aspect of the trauma."[49] This can be seen through the lack of memory to recall a particular battle or even periods of time that they cannot remember who died or became injured.

(4) "markedly diminished interest or participation in significant activities."[50] This would be marked by what the person did before the onset of PTSD compared to what they do presently such as staying home watching TV and giving up activities such as hunting or going places where there are crowds.

(5) "feelings of detachment or estrangement from others"[51] such as when one thinks that nobody can understand what it's like or that he/she is on the outside

---

[49] *Id.*

[50] *Id.*

[51] *Id.*

looking in at others and feel like they do not care about other things or people the way they used too.

(6) "restricted range of affect such as unable to have loving feelings"[52] unable to cry when loved ones die or do not feel love for one's spouse.

(7) "sense of a foreshortened future"[53] such as not expecting to have a career, marriage, children, or a long-life span[54] or they are afraid to commit to something or someone on a permanent basis.

The Diagnostic criterion in section 309.81, DSM-IV, goes on the state:[55]

D. "Persistent symptoms of increased arousal (not present before the trauma), as indicated by two (or more) of the following:"[56]

---

[52] *Id.*

[53] *Id.*

[54] *Id.*

[55] *Id.*

[56] *Id.*

(1) "difficulty falling or staying asleep"[57]

(2) "irritability or outbursts of anger"[58]

(3) "difficulty concentrating"[59] such as reading a page and unable to remember what was just read, forgetting what your spouse or co-worker just told you. One can also feel dumb because they do not follow conversations or just can't focus.

(4) "hypervigilance"[60] such as always looking for danger, worrying about people getting hurt, still looking for tripwires and sitting with your back to the wall, avoiding crowds, etc.

---

[57] *Id.*

[58] *Id.*

[59] *Id.*

[60] *Id.*

(5) "exaggerated startle response"[61] such as dropping to the ground at the sound of a backfire or loud noise and the person can't be touched when asleep, etc.

E. "Duration of the disturbance (symptoms in Criteria B, C, and D) is more than 1 month."[62]

F. "The disturbance causes clinically significant distress or impairment in social, occupational, or other important areas of functioning."[63] These must be specified if diagnosed as "acute if the duration of the symptoms is less than three months"[64] or "chronic if the duration of symptoms is three months or more."[65] These disturbances can be

---

[61] *Id.*

[62] *Id.*

[63] *Id.*

[64] *Id.*

[65] *Id.*

classified as a delayed onset if the onset of the symptoms is at least six months after the stressor.[66]

By utilizing the above listed criteria when diagnosing military veterans who claim to be suffering from PTSD, the American Psychiatric Association has estimated that that over eight percent of the American population currently suffers from PTSD and that they will have a lifetime prevalence of this disorder.[67] Among this statement, the highest rates among those will come from combat veterans who served in or are currently serving in a military combat operation.[68] With the enormous number of American troops returning from Afghanistan and Iraq within the next few years,[69] that percentage will definitely increase.

---

[66] *Id.*

[67] VETERANS DISABILITY BENEFITS COMMISSION, *supra* note 3, at 466.

[68] *Id.*

[69] VETERANS DISABILITY BENEFITS COMMISSION, *supra* note 3, at 383.

Other factors can increase the probability of acquiring PTSD, such as family history, severity of the stressor, proximity to the event, childhood experiences and preexisting mental conditions. When these indicators exist and when they are combined with exposure to trauma, this can exacerbate its severity.[70] Existing evidence also suggests that PTSD can be inherited.[71] However, "[this disorder can develop in individuals without any predisposing conditions, particularly if the stressor is especially extreme."[72] In short, there is no profile of a person who may or may not develop PTSD.

In short, there is no profile of a person who may or may not develop PTSD. A person exposed to trauma can be subject to its debilitating symptoms and another person may be able to resist.[73]

---

[70] AMERICAN PSYCHIATRIC ASSOCIATION, *supra* note 40, at 466

[71] *Id.* at 466-67.

[72] *Id.*

[73] Garcia-Rill & Beecher-Monas, *supra* note 30, at 19.

With regard to combat military personnel, new and varied U.S. military missions have a great impact on a service member or veterans' psyche. In particular, the "diversity in the nature and character of the missions" created a vast difference in combat experiences for veterans.[74] Research trends have proven that veterans tend to engage in crime because of the survival mode derived from combat.[75] Because of this, evaluators of PTSD have prepared new assessment instruments to "account for the changing nature of the mission" (i.e., changing from a peacekeeping mission to a combat mission or changing from a mission to remove a dictator to a defense mission).[76] Evaluators now take into consideration the environment, the person's emotional responses, what type of military activities they participated

---

[74] John P. Wilson & Terence M. Keane, *Assessing Psychological Trauma and PTSD*, 259, (2d ed.1997).

[75] *Id.* at 278.

[76] Id. at 279.

in and the dimensions of the mission itself.[77] The dimensions of the mission will help determine which stressors may be present.[78]

In a 1983, John P. Wilson and Sheldon D. Zigelbaum conducted a study of 114 Vietnam veterans which revealed that a survival instinct manifests itself in three modes: 1) the dissociative reaction, 2) the sensation seeking syndrome and 3) the depression-suicide syndrome.[79]

The most prevalent symptom is dissociation reaction because this symptom causes the veteran to believe that they are in active combat and must respond to perceived stressors with violence as they would have in true combat.[80] Because of this survivor-mode reaction, PTSD is commonly associated with violent criminal behavior.[81]

---

[77] Id.

[78] Id.

[79] John P. Wilson & Sheldon D. Zigelbaum, The Vietnam Veteran on Trial: The Relation of Post-Traumatic Stress Disorder to Criminal Behavior, 1 BEHAV. SCI. & L., VOL. 69, 73-76 (1983).

[80] *Id.* at 73.

[81] *Id.*

However, PTSD can also be associated with non-violent criminal activities because of the sensation seeking syndrome.[82]

The syndrome causes veterans to engage in dangerous and thrilling behavior in order to maintain control over the traumatic imagery they are experiencing. "[It performs a defensive function since the sensation seeking syndrome is a complex form of repetition compulsion which blocks the onset of intrusive experiences."[83] This means that if the veteran does not fulfill this sensation, he or she begins to suffer the extreme symptoms of PTSD.[84]

---

[82] *Id.* at 74.

[83] *Id.*

[84] *Id.*

Finally, the survivor-mode may cause the veteran to experience the depression-suicide syndrome. Here, the veteran is plagued by depression, guilt that he survived, and his fellow troop members did not, and a sense that he was a mere pawn used by the government.[85] Because of these rampant feelings of self-loathing and depression, the service member or veteran may seek to take his or her own life as a way to end the terrible memories he or she is experiencing or to join his or her departed service members.[86] "Such a suicidal wish may then give rise to criminal action if the veteran unconsciously acts out his anger at the government or other authority figures symbolically equivalent."[87]

---

[85] *Id.* at 75.

[86] *Id.*

[87] *Id.*

Considering the current opposition to the war in Afghanistan and Iraq, this syndrome may be the most frequent among those veterans returning from a tour of duty in these locations.[88] Thus, PTSD may present itself in many forms, all equally devastating and all equally dangerous. Knowledge of the disorder and its symptoms may provide the military member or veteran an appropriate defense in a criminal prosecution.[89]

---

[88] Grover, *supra* note 6, at 568.

[89] *Id.*

CHAPTER 7

Proving Post-Traumatic Stress Disorder

Surveys of service personnel reveal some of the circumstances that contribute to the development of PTSD. These include: "being attacked or ambushed, . . . being shot at or receiving small arms fire, . . . seeing dead bodies or human remains, . . . knowing someone else seriously injured or killed, . . . seeing ill or injured women or children whom they were unable to help, . . . [having] a buddy shot or hit who was near them, . . . and engaging in hand-to-hand combat."[90]

A study of nearly 3,000 Iraq War veterans found killing in combat a significant predictor of PTSD and suggests that taking a life in combat is a potent ingredient in the development of mental health difficulties"[91]

---

[90] Nidiffer & Leach, *supra* note 37, at 351.

[91] Shira Maguen, Barbara A. Lucenko, Mark A. Reger, Gregory A. Gahm, Brett T. Litz, Karen H. Seal, Sara J. Knight, & Charles R. Marmar, *The Impact of Reported Direct and Indirect Killing on Mental Health Symptoms in Iraq War Veterans*, 23, J. OF TRAUMATIC STRESS, 86 (February 2010).

and that killing "was also a significant predictor of . . . anger and relationship difficulties."[92] Another study suggests that service personnel with "higher levels of exposure to violent combat, who had killed another person" were more likely to engage in risky behaviors, which may include excessive alcohol use, use of illicit drugs, and violent behavior.[93] Military mental health officials have found that among personnel deployed to Afghanistan and Iraq, lengthy deployments, multiple redeployments, and little "down time" between deployments contributed directly to the development of mental health conditions.[94]

---

[92] *Id.* at 86-87.

[93] William D.S. Killgore, Dave I. Cotting, Jeffrey L. Thomas, Anthony L. Cox, Dennis McGurk, Alexander H. Vo, Carl A. Castro & Charles W. Hoge, *Post-combat Invincibility: Violent Combat Experiences Are Associated with Increased Risk-Taking Propensity Following Deployment,* 42(13) J. OF PSYCHIATRIC RESEARCH, 1112 (Oct. 2008).

[94] THE CENTER FOR MENTAL HEALTH SERVICES GAINS CENTER, U.S. DEPT. OF HEALTH AND HUMAN SERVICES, SUBSTANCE ABUSE AND MENTAL HEALTH SERVICES ADMINISTRATION, RESPONDING TO THE NEEDS OF JUSTICE INVOLVED COMBAT VETERANS WITH SERVICE-RELATED TRAUMA AND MENTAL HEALTH CONDITIONS: A CONSENSUS REPORT OF THE CMHS NATIONAL GAINS CENTER'S FORUM ON COMBAT VETERANS, TRAUMA, AND THE JUSTICE SYSTEM, available at http://www.gainscenter.samhsa.gov/text/veterans/ Responding_to_Needs_8_08.asp (last visited September 13, 2012).

There is a general agreement that PTSD is considered "dose-dependent."[95] In other words, the greater the exposure to traumatic events, the more severe the symptoms will be.[96] However, the relationship between these factors and the development and severity of PTSD in today's veteran population remains unclear.

Both the Veterans Administration and the National Institute of Mental Health provide ongoing and updated information specific to PTSD through their general web sites, official journals and pamphlets.[97]

It is extremely harsh for the courts to hold defendants liable by imposing the death penalty when their crimes would likely not have happened but for their military service and service-related injuries.[98]

---

[95] THE OFFICE OF GENERAL COUNSEL, *supra* note 1, at 3.

[96] Norman Poythress, Christopher Slobogin, Tomika K. Stevens & Kirk Heilbrun, § 9:37. *Posttraumatic Stress Disorder – Areas of Scientific Agreement*, 2 MODERN SCIENTIFIC EVIDENCE: THE LAW AND SCIENCE OF EXPERT TESTIMONY, 2005-2006.

[97] THE OFFICE OF GENERAL COUNSEL, *supra* note 1, at 4.

[98] Hal S. Wortzel & David B. Arcineigas, *Combat Veterans and the Death Penalty; A Forensic Neuropsychiatric Perspective,* J AM ACAD PSYCHIATRY LAW, 38: 407-414, (2010).

However, despite this, some service members and veterans could possibly face execution when prosecutors choose to seek the death penalty, and when judges and juries find them responsible for their crimes and to be without enough significant mitigating circumstances to spare their lives.[99]

PTSD has been a tragic consequence of exposure to combat for veterans of every war and other military actions. The increasing numbers of service members who return home to the United States with combat involvement from war zones in Afghanistan and Iraq have been accompanied by an increase in the population that suffers from PTSD.[100]

With a clinical definition and diagnosis of PTSD, it can be shown that service members and veterans, if clinically diagnosed are truly suffering from this disorder, should be classified as mentally unstable and hence, the death penalty should be considered to be cruel and unusual as outlined in

---

[99] Hannah Loomer-Johnson, *Veterans and the Death Penalty: Defending the Lives of Veterans with Post-Traumatic Stress Disorder*, 1 (2011).

[100] Daniel Burgess, *Reviving the "Vietnam Defense": Post-Traumatic Stress Disorder and Criminal Responsibility in A Post-Iraq/Afghanistan World*, 29 DEV. MENTAL HEALTH L. 59-60 (2010).

past case law as well as the U.S. Constitution's Eighth Amendment. The U.S. Supreme Court has recently noted the nation's military as a "long tradition of according leniency to veterans in recognition of their service, especially for those who fought on the front lines."[101] If the courts have remarked that some form of leniency could be shown to military members, it can be proven that the death penalty should be deemed cruel and unusual punishment and spare these soldiers from such a sentence.

In November 2011, the Veterans Affairs (VA) reported that of the more than estimated 1.5 million combat veterans who have participated in Afghanistan and Iraq, the VA has treated 211,819 soldiers for PTSD.[102] According to the VA, these numbers do not include those individuals who suffer from PTSD, and either seek treatment elsewhere in the private sector or do not seek treatment at all.[103]

---

[101] *Id.*

[102] David G. Young, N.D., *Post-Traumatic Stress Disorder (PTSD)*, available at http://www.naturopathic-physician.com/index.php? Page =86 (last visited Oct. 1, 2012).

[103] *Id.*

Due to the stress of combat of service members, researchers have noted that there are strong connections between military combat service and conditions such as PTSD, anxiety and depressive disorders, and substance abuse.[104] With the introduction of Improvised Explosive Devices (IED'S), this has brought on a large number of military members returning with traumatic brain injuries (TBI) and PTSD.[105] While it is commonly accepted that overall combat experience can be linked to the start of some mental conditions, it is well-known that a TBI can affect ones normal brain function and ultimately their behavior.[106] Although, there is still a wide debate over what causes individuals to develop PTSD and what behavioral issues result from a TBI.[107]

---

[104] *Id.*

[105] THE OFFICE OF GENERAL COUNSEL, *supra* note 1, at 2.

[106] *Id.*

[107] *Id.*

Given the aggressive behavior control issues that are common with this disorder, it is not surprising that there is an alarming increase of veterans facing the death penalty is one of important significance, especially when it involves a combat veteran who suffered from PTSD at the time of the incident.

<h1>CHAPTER 8</h1>

Mental Illnesses and the Death Penalty

Throughout our legal history, there have been numerous cases wherein a defendant asserts that he or she is mentally insane and should be consider not guilty by reason of insanity. There have been several formulas of the insanity defense over the course of history and its definition continues to vary state by state.[108] The McNaughton Rule, also commonly known as the right and wrong test, states that an accused must not be held criminally liable if he "at the time of committing the act, the accused was laboring under such a defect of reason, from disease of the mind, as not to know the nature and quality of the act he was doing or, if he did know it, that he did not know what he was doing was wrong."[109]

---

[108] Debra D. Burke & Mary Anne Nixon, *Post-Traumatic Stress Disorder and the Death Penalty,* 38 How. L.J., 183, 184 (1994).

[109] Cornell University Law School, Legal Information Institute, Insanity Defense, available at http://www.law.cornell.edu/wex/ins.insanity_defense (last visited (last visited Sept. 25, 2012

Within the United States, various courts supplement the right and wrong inquiry of the McNaughton Rule with the Irresistible Impulse Test, which considers whether the defendant, because of a disease of the mind, was unable to control the impulse to do wrong.[110] Additionally, a third test for insanity, as referred to as the Durham or product test, states that a defendant should not be liable if the criminal offense was the product of a mental disease or defect.[111] If presented, this argument by the defense is very reliant upon the presentation of expert testimony due to its connection in defining insanity.[112]

Accordingly, Post-Traumatic Stress Disorder should almost certainly be considered a valid insanity defense only if the degree of dysfunction was found to be overwhelming. In cases of severe impairment, it could be argued that PTSD sufferers, "as a result of mental disease, are unable to

---

[110] Burke & Nixon, *supra* note 108, at 191.

[111] *Id.*

[112] *Id.*

appreciate the wrongfulness of their acts or to conform their actions to lawful requirements."[113] For example, a service member who mentally re-lives a war time experience where the act or killing or be killed was performed, or at the least expected of that soldier, may not be able to comprehend that a current act of killing is considered to be wrong. The significance of this issue is obviously greater in cases involving combat service members who commit a capital offense and face the death penalty.[114] This issue is also relevant in respect to current death row inmates who have either failed to successfully utilize the insanity defense at trial or have been unsuccessful in asserting PTSD as a basis for their insanity defense.

---

[113] Burke & Nixon, *supra* note 108, at 192.

[114] *Id.*

The Law and PTSD

Capital punishment does not violate the Eighth Amendment's prohibition against cruel and unusual punishment.[115] Capital punishment became a viable option when the Bill of Rights was ratified in 1791.[116] At a minimum, the Amendment prohibited punishment that was considered to be cruel and unusual and was an effort to restrict the definition as such "a static moment in history would be analytically unsound."[117]

Consequently, the exclusion also recognizes "evolving

---

[115] *Furman v. Georgia*, 408 U.S. 238 (1972) "Excessive bail shall not be required, nor excessive fines imposed, nor cruel and unusual punishments inflicted." U.S. Const. amend. VIII. As the Fourteenth Amendment has been interpreted, the Eighth Amendment is binding upon the states.

[116] William J. Brennan, Jr., *Constitutional Adjudication and the Death Penalty: A View from the Court,* 100 HARV. L. REV. 313, 323-24 (1986).

[117] Burke & Nixon, *supra* note 108, at 192.

standards of decency that mark the progress of a maturing society."[118] If legislative laws as well as the federal government, the military and forty-one states allow capital punishment, then this could help prove a "norm" of decency and one could conclude that society agrees that executions serve the dual purposes of retribution and deterrence.[119] Cases involving combat veterans who suffer from PTSD may be very significant where capital cases utilize this disorder as mitigating circumstances. It wasn't until the 1970's that the death penalty was seriously challenged when Furman v. Georgia,[120] came to light. In this case, the defendant had been sentenced to death after being convicted of murder when he accidentally shot a homeowner while attempting to burglarize the residence.[121]

---

[118] *Id.*

[119] *Gregg v. Georgia*, 428 U.S. 153, 179-83 (1976). The Supreme Court recognizes that society values and justifies capital punishment because of its deterrence value and retribution characteristic. This view is reflected in legislative enactments and public opinion polls.

[120] *Furman v. Georgia*, 408 U.S. 238 (1972).

[121] *Id.*

After a direct review had failed, the defendant filed a writ of certiorari to the United States Supreme Court of Georgia.

Upon granting certiorari, the Court found that the key question was whether the imposition and carrying out of the death penalty under the laws applicable to the defendant constituted cruel and unusual punishment in violation of the Eighth and Fourteenth Amendments.[122] In reversing the lower courts' judgment, the Court held that the death penalty did violate the Eighth and Fourteenth Amendments because the application of the penalty was discretionary, haphazard, and discriminatory in that it was inflicted in a small number of the total possible cases and primarily against certain minority groups.[123]

---

[122] *Id.*

[123] *Id.*

Due to the Court's ruling in Furman, it is possible to show that if service members who suffers from combat related PTSD at the time of committing a capital offense, is also "a small number of the total possible cases and primarily against certain minority groups" and should not be sentenced to the death penalty. Furthermore, when examining combat service members and veterans who claim to suffer from PTSD and face capital punishment, one can study the ruling by the U.S. Supreme Court in Lockett v. Ohio.[124] In this case, the Supreme Court ruled that the Eighth Amendment to the U.S. Constitution required that the jury "not be precluded from considering as a mitigating factor, any aspect of the defendants character or record and any of the circumstances of the offense that the defendant proffers as a basis for a sentence less than death."[125]

---

[124] *Lockett v. Ohio*, 438 U.S. 586 (1978).

[125] *Id.* at 604. The Ohio statute which was struck down in Lockett required that a defendant be sentenced to death for aggravated murder unless one of three specific mitigating circumstances was present.

Such mitigating evidence can include not only the circumstances surrounding the offense, but also qualities of the defendant's character, background, record, emotional disturbance, or troubled family history.[126]

Lockett was convicted of aggravated murder and sentenced to the death penalty in connection with a robbery and murder during which she waited in the getaway car she was driving. The State Supreme Court affirmed her conviction and sentence.[127] On her petition for further review, the Supreme Court reversed the death sentence, holding that the Ohio death penalty statute violated the Eighth which prohibits cruel and unusual punishment.[128] This was because the court did not permit the jury to consider a necessary range of mitigating factors, including the defendant's character, age, record, or the circumstances of the offense.

---

[126] Burke & Nixon, *supra* note 108, at 197.

[127] *Lockett,* 438 U.S. at 604

[128] *Id.*

The Court ruled that the statute was unconstitutionally narrow where it imposed a mandatory death sentence based on a finding that the victim did not induce the offense, that the defendant did not act under duress or coercion, and that the crime was not the product of the victim's mental deficiency.[129]

This case can also be utilized in today's courts where veterans are receiving the death penalty. As in Lockett, if the court reversed the penalty due to not permitting the jury to consider a necessary range of mitigating factors to include the defendant's character, age, record, or the circumstances of the offense, this could be true with a veteran suffering from PTSD at the time of the crime. The veteran's character, record and the circumstances surrounding the crime need to be taken into account and utilized as mitigating circumstances to relieve them of the death penalty.

---

[129] *Id.*

Notwithstanding the above cases, the landmark case which defines the execution of mentally retarded persons as unconstitutional stems from Atkins v. Virginia.[130] In this case Daryl Atkins was found guilty of the murder of Eric Nesbitt in 1996 and was sentenced to the death penalty.

Atkins challenged the State Supreme Court of Virginia citing that his sentence was unconstitutional because he was "mentally retarded and thus [could not] be sentenced to death."[131] In a divided opinion, the court relied on Penry v. Lynaugh, 492 U.S. 302 (1989), to hold that mentally retarded persons could be sentenced to death.[132]

In granting certiorari, the United States Supreme Court addressed "the gravity of the concerns expressed by the dissenters" from the lower court and readdressed the main

---

[130] Atkins v. Virginia, 534 S.E.2d 312 (2000); Anthony E., Giardino, Combat Veterans, Mental Health Issues, and the Death Penalty: Addressing the Impact of Post-Traumatic Stress Disorder and Traumatic Brain Injury, 77 Fordham L. Rev. 2955 (2009).

[131] *Atkins,* 534 S.E.2d at 318; Giardino, *supra* note 130, at 2984-85.

[132] *Atkins*, 534 S.E.2d at 319; Giardino, *supra* note 130, at 2984-85; Douglas Mossman, *Atkins v. Virginia: A Psychiatric Can of Worms,* 33 N.M. L. REV. 255 (2003).

issue in Penry regarding the constitutionality of imposing the death penalty upon a mentally retarded person.[133] In their ruling, the Supreme Court opined that the mentally retarded cannot be subjected to the death penalty and ruled that "[if]f the culpability of the average murderer is insufficient to justify the most extreme sanction available to the State, the lessor culpability of the mentally retarded offender surely does not merit that form of retribution."[134]

The Court also ruled that the mentally impaired are warranted to a categorical exclusion from the death penalty due to a national consensus that had changed regarding the "relative culpability of mentally retarded offenders," the lack of satisfaction of the "penological" goals of the death penalty in executing the mentally impaired, the mitigating nature of the characteristics of mental retardation, and the "risk 'that the death penalty will be imposed in spite of

---

[133] *Atkins v. Virginia,* 536 U.S. 304, at 310 (2002); Giardino, *supra* note 130, at 2984-85; Helen Shin, *Is the Death of the Death Penalty Near? The Impact of Atkins and Roper on the future of capital punishment for Mentally Ill Defendants,* 76 FORDHAM L. REV. 465 (2007).

[134] *Atkins,* 536 U.S. at 319; Giardino, *supra* note 130, at 2984-85.

factors which may call for a less severe penalty.[135]

In reviewing this case, the Court determined that the distinctive mark of contemporary values, combined with the morals of society, reflected uneasiness with the intolerance for the execution of mentally impaired defendants. [136]

The Court discovered that in the years following Penry v. Lynaugh, a national consent had developed which had been centered on the actions of legislatures that "unquestionably reflected a widespread judgment about the relative culpability of mentally retarded offenders, and the relationship between mental retardation and the penological purposes served by the death penalty."[137]

---

[135] *Atkins*, 536 U.S. at 317, 320 (quoting *Lockett v. Ohio*, 438 U.S. 586, 605 (1978)); Giardino, *supra* note 130, at 2984-85.

[136] *Atkins*, 536 U.S. at 313-17; Giardino, *supra* note 130, at 2984-85; Shin, *supra* note 133, at 478-80.

[137] *Atkins*, 536 U.S. at 317; Giardino, *supra* note 130, at 2984-85; Shin, *supra* note 133, at 47.

After the Court had objective evidence that indicated that there was a national consensus against the imposition of the death penalty on the mentally impaired, the Court then moved onto another step where they had to analyze and examine the issue utilizing its own independent judgment.[138]

During this examination, the Court reviewed the penological goals of the death penalty and discovered that neither deterrence nor retribution was advanced in executing the mentally impaired.[139] The Court ruled that the retributive purpose of the death penalty was not correctly served in this instance because, "if the execution was an improper punishment for the average offender, it was most certainly inappropriate in because, "if the execution was an improper punishment for the average

---

[138] *Atkins*, 536 U.S. at 317-21; Giardino, *supra* note 130, at 2984-85; Shin, *supra* note 133, at 480-81.

[139] *Atkins*, 536 U.S. at 319; Giardino, *supra* note 130, at 2984-85; Shin, *supra* note 133, at 480.

offender, it was most certainly inappropriate in the case involving a mentally retarded person."[140]

The Court reasoned that the deterrent purposes of the death penalty were not advanced because it was "less likely that [the mentally retarded] can process the information of the possibility of execution as a penalty and, as a result, control their conduct based upon that information."[141]

The court further discovered that mentally impaired individuals "by definition . . . have diminished capacities to understand and process information, to communicate, to abstract from mistakes and learn from experience, to engage in logical reasoning, to control impulses, and to understand the reactions of others."[142]

---

[140] *Atkins,* 536 U.S. at 318-320; Giardino, *supra* note 130, at 2984-85; Shin, *supra* note 133, at 480.

Atkins, 536 U.S. at 320; Giardino, *supra* note 130, at 2985; Shin, *supra* note 133, at 480.

[142] *Atkins,* 536 U.S. at 18.

Lastly, the Court realized that there was an unacceptable risk where evidence of mental retardation presented in mitigation had the possibility of being misconstrued by a jury as a factor in aggravation despite the fact that it should call for a penalty less severe than death.[143]

More pertinent to PTSD and the death penalty is the execution of death row inmates who suffer from this disorder, yet stand to be executed and whether this violate the Constitution and the Eighth Amendment's cruel and unusual clause.[144] The prohibition against executing a mentally insane person can be found deep-rooted within the common law.[145] This exclusion is justified because the primary goals of capital punishment, retribution and deterrence, cannot be furthered by executing one who is

---

[143] *Atkins,* 536 U.S. at 320-21; Giardino, *supra* note 130, at 2985; Shin, *supra* note 133, at 481.

[144] *Atkins,* 536 U.S. at 320-21; Giardino, *supra* note 130, at 2985; Shin, *supra* note 133, at 481.

[145] Jonathan L. Entin, *Psychiatry, Insanity, and the Death Penalty: A Note on Implementing Supreme Court Decisions,* 79 CRIM. L. & CRIMINOLOGY 218, 220 (1988).

insane since the individual has no emotional or intellectual understanding of the punishment, and the only possible deterred class, incompetents, cannot comprehend the lesson.[146]

This common law prohibition was elevated to a constitutional one in Ford v. Wainwright,[147] where the Court held that execution of an inmate who becomes insane after conviction constitutes cruel and unusual punishment. Justice Powell, in his concurring opinion, defined this competency requirement as being an awareness by the prisoner of the impending execution and the reason for it; however, the Court did not formulate any procedural requirements for determining this issue.[148]

---

[146] Matthew S. Collins, Note, *Involuntarily Medicating Condemned Incompetents For The Purpose Of Rendering Them Sane And Thereby Subject To Execution*, 70 WASH. U. L. Q. 1237-47 (1992).

[147] *Ford v. Wainwright*, 477 U.S. 399 (1986).

[148] *Id.* at 410-15.

Justice Powell continued by suggesting that the safeguards could be less formal than those of a trial, yet still allow for an impartial decision maker to evaluate the expert psychiatric evidence presented by the defense and the prosecution.[149] In the end, it was decided that whatever procedure is utilized in the future, the critical point for resolving the issue of competence of an inmate should be the time appointed for execution.[150]

The Supreme Court ruled that the act of forcing medication on a prisoner in order to restore competency for the purpose of an execution violated the state's constitution.[151] The United States Supreme Court has ruled that inmates may be treated with antipsychotic drugs in appropriate circumstances[152] but has not determined whether execution is such a circumstance.[153]

---

[149] *Id.* at 427.

[150] *Id.* At 429.

[151] *Id.* at 771.

[152] *Washington v. Harper*, 494 U.S. 210 (1990).

[153] Collins, *supra* note 146, at 1244-45.

The test for competency to execute prisoners is quite different from the test in determining one's capacity in order to stand trial and is also different for the test of an individual's sanity at the time the offense was committed. Incompetency for execution appears to require the greatest impairment of reasoning.[154] Experts have testified that the most likely mental infirmities to cause such an extreme cognitive dis-function are organic mental disorders and syndromes, as well as certain psychoses such as paranoid schizophrenia.[155] Subsequently, only a very severe case of PTSD, which deteriorated during the defendant's incarceration could actually satisfy this requirement.[156]

---

[154] Burke & Nixon, *supra* note 108, at 196.

[155] Donald H. Wallace, *The Need To Commute the Death Sentence: Competency For Execution and Ethical Dilemmas For Mental Health Professionals*, 15 INTL. J. L. PSYCH. 317, 319 (1992).

[156] Burke & Nixon, *supra* note 108, at 196.

CHAPTER **10**

The Significance of Post-Traumatic Stress Disorder in Capital Cases

As stated earlier in this study, PTSD should be an extremely significant matter in capital cases which can be uses as a mitigating circumstance. In Furman, the Court held that it was a requirement that a jury be given guidelines for their determination of whether to impose the death penalty.[157] In response to the Court's decision, States approved death penalty statutes which narrowed the potential class of capital defendants by requiring the consideration of aggravating circumstances, such as if the crime was especially cruel, heinous or atrocious.[158]

Disorders which hinder the mental capacity and can affect a person's state of mind should be considered mitigating circumstances during the sentencing phase.

---

[157] *Furman,* 408 U.S. at 313.

[158] *Profitt v. Florida*, 428 U.S. 242, 245 (1976); *Woodson v. North Carolina*, 428 U.S. 280 (1976); *Zant v. Stephens*, 462 U.S. 862 (1983).

In Penry v. Lynaugh,[159] the Supreme Court held that a finding of mental retardation alone did not justify a blanket exemption from the death penalty, because there was no national consensus against the execution of mentally retarded defendants.[160] The Court also determined that because only two states ban the execution of retarded individual's, such punishment could not be considered cruel and unusual under the Eighth Amendment.[161] Nevertheless, the Court did hold that the special instructions given to the jury did not allow for an adequate consideration of the defendant's mental retardation as a mitigating circumstance.[162]

---

[159] *Penry v. Lynaugh,* 492 U.S. 302 (1989).

[160] *Id.* at 334.

[161] *Id.* at 335.

[162] *Id.* at 337.

If PTSD does not support an insanity defense or even an argument in favor of insanity so as to bar execution, PTSD should be considered as a mitigating factor where the death penalty should be ruled as cruel and unusual under the Eighth Amendment, just as in the case of mentally impaired people.

In California's first review of the evidence in a capital case involving a Vietnam veteran who suffered from PTSD, the State Supreme Court reversed the death sentence of Philip Lucero in People v. Lucero.[163] In this case, the trial court had excluded expert testimony that Lucero might have committed murder in a delayed reaction to war-time trauma. "[Lucero] was entitled to have the jury consider his psychological disorder as a factor in mitigation, whether or not the mental condition caused him to commit the crimes."[164]

---

[163] *People v. Lucero*, 750 P.2d 1342 (Ca. 1988).

[164] *Lucero*, 750 P.2d. at 1356.

In another state, the Utah Supreme Court previously allowed testimony of PTSD as a mitigating factor in the trial of Steven Ray Stout. In his testimony concerning the murders of two women, Stout claimed he was unable to remember anything about the killings, and he expressed a desire to get therapy so he could understand his actions. With this testimony taken into consideration, the aggravating factors failed to outweigh the mitigating factors making the imposition of the death penalty unjustified and inappropriate.[165]

The Supreme Court favors finality in sentences imposed by competent state courts. It generally prohibits new constitutional rules of criminal conduct from applying retroactively to cases on collateral review. A new rule may apply retroactively, however, if the rule places certain kinds

---

[165] Stephen Hunt, "*Shell-Shocked' Stout Won't Die for Crimes*", Salt Lake Trib., Nov. 16, 1989, at A1. A clinical psychologist specializing in PTSD testified that, although PTSD is usually associated with war, it is also known to be produced by a variety of traumatic experiences. In this particular case the defense was extended to include PTSD resulting from childhood trauma. Stout and his siblings suffered physical and emotional abuse at the hands of an older brother in one room of their childhood home known as "the torture chamber."

of primary private individual conduct beyond the power of the criminal lawmaking authority to proscribe or requires the observance of procedures implicit in the concept of ordered liberty.[166]

A case can only announce a new rule if it meets one of three criteria: (1) if the case breaks new ground; (2) if it imposes a new obligation on the government; or (3) if the result was not dictated by precedent at the time the conviction became final.[167]

Therefore, if a defendant's conviction became final prior to 1978 when the Court decided Lockett v. Ohio,[168] (which required mitigating factors to be considered) it could not have this new rule applied unless the case fell into one of the two exceptions. Arguably, the second exception might apply since the refusal of such consideration would result

---

[166] Burke & Nixon, *supra* note 108, at 191; *Teague v. Lane*, 489 U.S. 288, 305-10 (1988).

[167] *Teague*, 489 U.S. at 301.

[168] *Lockett,* 438 U.S. at 586.

in the imposition of cruel and unusual punishment and the right to be free from such punishment is fundamental.

Nevertheless, the defendants whose convictions became final after Lockett was decided should have enjoyed the benefit of that decision and a new trial on the issue of punishment should have been granted.[169]

---

[169] *Penry*, 492 U.S. at 314-19 (states cannot prevent the jury from considering and giving effect to evidence relevant to the defendant's background or character which mitigates against imposing the death penalty).

CHAPTER 11

The Courts View of Military Service and Veterans

The courts recognize that mental illnesses can limit a person's capacity to act responsibly. Because the American Psychiatric Association has deemed PTSD as a mental condition, the courts have come to recognize that this disorder can diminish a person's mental capacity.[170]A capital case that reached the United States Supreme Court brings the issues of leniency towards veterans and the effect combat can have on mental health into sharp focus.

In Porter v.McCullom,[171] the Supreme Court considered the defendant's conviction and death sentence for fatally shooting his former girlfriend and her boyfriend. In holding that the defendant's trial counsel had rendered ineffective assistance by failing to investigate or present mitigating

---

[170] *Id.*

[171] *Porter v. McCollum*, 130 S.Ct. 447 (2009).

evidence about, among other things, the defendant's military record, the Court described Porter's military record:[172]Petitioner George Porter is a veteran who was both wounded and decorated for his active participation in two major engagements in the Korean War; his combat service unfortunately left him a traumatized, changed man.[173] The Court observed that, had Porter's counsel been effective in presenting mitigating evidence, the judge and jury would have learned of the 'kind of troubled history we have declared relevant to assessing a defendant's moral culpability.' They would have heard about (1) Porter's

---

[172] *Id.*

[173] *Id.* at 448.

heroic military service in two of the most critical – and horrific – battles of the Korean War, (2) his struggles to regain normality upon his return from war, (3) his childhood history of physical abuse, and (4) his brain abnormality, difficulty reading and writing, and limited schooling."[174]

The Court emphasized the importance of Porter's military service as a mitigating factor, stating, "[o]our Nation has a long tradition of according leniency to veterans in recognition of their service, especially for those who fought on the front lines as did Porter.[175] Moreover, the relevance of Porter's extensive combat experience is not only that he served honorably under extreme hardship and gruesome conditions, but also that the jury might find mitigating the intense stress and mental and emotional toll that combat took on Porter."[176]

---

[174] *Id.* at 454 (quoting Wiggins v. Smith, 539 U.S. 510, 535 (2003)).

[175] *Id.*

[176] *Id.*

It can be argued that the primary difficulty for attorneys in all PTSD defense cases is the manner in which the disorder is proven.[177] The successfulness of any PTSD case is dependent upon the method of proof provided to the court.[178] As the mental state is always a main issue in any criminal case, expert proof of PTSD should demonstrate to address whether or not the individual was or was not culpable. To show this, attorneys must prove PTSD factually, using detailed exhibits and testimony that describe the trauma incurred.[179]

For a war veteran, this could include various types of evidence such as testimony from members of the defendant's military unit that was present at the time of the trauma, testimony from military commanders who can provide details of the mission and prior intelligence,

---

[177] Grover, supra note 6, at 568.

[178] *Id.*

[179] *Id.*

military records and personal testimony from outside the

provide details of the mission and prior intelligence,

military records and personal testimony from outside the

military concerning the defendant's behavior before and

after the tour of duty.[180]

The facts proven would then apply towards one of the

defenses applicable to mental state (insanity, diminished

capacity, self-defense, etc.). PTSD is the one psychological

disorder that can be proven absolutely, because it stems

from an identifiable trauma and the evidence of that trauma

is discernible.[181] Therefore, PTSD, if properly proven, has

the absolute potential to be successful regardless of the

defense used.[182]

---

[180] *Id.*

[181] *Id.*

[182] *Id.*

However, it can also be argued that even if PTSD is proven, the inadequacies in the legal standards and defenses still pose a barrier to PTSD defense success. The trauma suffered by a war veteran may be admissible, but it is ultimately up to the fact finder to determine if that trauma sufficiently qualifies for an insanity defense, diminished capacity, self- defense, unconsciousness, and so on.[183]

The trauma qualifies if it affects the mental state to the extent prescribed by statute in order to negate mens rea. A veteran may well have suffered trauma, but a judge or jury may not see it as enough to cause the symptoms purported, and thus affect the men's rea to the extent necessary to reduce culpability.[184] A defense designed to encompass the symptoms of PTSD specifically may solve this issue for the predicted Iraq war veteran cases.[185]

---

[183] *Id.* at 569.

[184] *Id.*

[185] *Id.*

In most federal level criminal cases, the courts may look to various sources to determine whether a defendant truly suffers from PTSD.[186] As with most medical treatment, sometimes professionals have to rely on the military members self-reporting of traumatic experiences and the symptoms that accompany those experiences.[187]

Within the criminal justice system and the context within it, formal testing can also be applicable in order to properly validate a veteran's claim of PTSD.[188] Finally, courts can also obtain personnel records from the National Personnel Records Center to verify combat exposure and number and length of combat tours via the veterans Department of Defense Form 214, commonly referred to as a certificate of discharge.

---

[186] THE OFFICE OF GENERAL COUNSEL, *supra* note 1, at 2.

[187] *Id.*

[188] Karl Kirkland, *Post-Traumatic Stress Disorder v. Pseudo Post-Traumatic Stress Disorder*, 56 A LA. LAW. 90, 92 (1995).

After the American Psychiatric Association officially recognized it as a mental disorder in 1980,[189] the number of veterans who utilized this disorder as a defense rose dramatically. Subject to the legal jurisdiction of the defendant, utilizing PTSD as a defense can be abused in an attempt to prove insanity, diminished capacity, unconsciousness/automatism, or self-defense. This disorder can also be utilized as proceedings.[190]

With this said, when a military member or veteran uses PTSD as a defense and is effective in proving his/her insanity, he or she would then be committed to a mental health institution.[191] Upon a productive unconsciousness defense, the member or veteran would receive a complete acquittal of all charges, as well as a member or veteran who claims some sort of diminished capacity, depending on the legal jurisdictions.[192]

---

[189] AMERICAN PSYCHIATRIC ASSOCIATION , *supra* note 40, at 236-39.

[190] Auberry, *supra* note 9, at 646.

[191] *Id.* at 665.

[192] *United States v. Fishman*, 743 F. Supp. 713, 721 (N.D. Cal. 1990).

For those veterans who choose to use the unconsciousness defense, this can only apply to those individuals who experience dissociative states.[193] It appears that even though a veteran who suffers from PTSD can use a wide range of defenses, none of these can actually address the symptoms and results of PTSD, and may ultimately result in a possible death sentence. It is this sentence that should be classified as cruel and unusual due to the mental instability of the veteran at the time of the offense.

Military members who return home following their service in a war-zone, who commit a capital offense and who truly suffer from PTSD, deserve the right to be punished solely to the extent that they are culpable for their actions during the alleged crime.[194] Because of the unique circumstances that veterans endure, a defense that addresses the symptoms and provides the appropriate treatment needs to be

---

[193] Elizabeth J. Delgado, *Vietnam Stress Syndrome and the Criminal Defendant,* 19 LOY. L.A. L. REV. 473, 484 (1986).

[194] Grover, *supra* note 6, at 563.

examined and recognized by the courts.[195]

Throughout our legal history, it has proven that the death penalty is a real possibility and should not be an outcome for these unique individuals who have been called upon by our nation to defend our nation and the freedoms we enjoy.

---

[195] *Id.*

CHAPTER **12**

ARGUING FOR AND DEFINING A CATEGORICAL EXCLUSION

Based on the rationales of the cases presented within this study, there must be a very narrow, categorical exclusion, for military members and combat veterans who suffer from service related PTSD at the time of their offense.[196] This exclusion would reflect a national consensus that has developed over time regarding the impropriety of sentencing these individuals to the death penalty.[197] The Courts have to recognize that the "penological" goals of the death penalty are not served by executing these offenders.[198]

---

[196] Giardino, *supra* note 130, at 2988.

[197] *Id.*

[198] *Id.* at 2984.

The Courts also have to acknowledge the significant mitigating nature of PTSD in veterans who have been trained to kill the enemy by our government and address the unacceptable risk that a jury could disregard mitigating evidence of military training and PTSD to impose the death penalty where it is unwarranted.[199] If a categorical exclusion were initiated, it would not excuse the actions of those who commit a capital offense, but merely limit the veterans' punishment to a term of years or life imprisonment with the possibility of parole and eliminate the death penalty.[200] Defining a categorical exclusion for veterans with service- related PTSD could pose some problems and draw some harsh critics; however, it is possible to create a clear definition and place very specific requirements on those who request this classification.[201]

---

[199] Giardino, *supra* note 130, at 2988.

[200] *Id.*

[201] *Id.*

Veterans would unquestionably have to have seen combat as defined by taking fire by the enemy or firing upon the enemy[202] while serving in a combat or peace keeping zone. Enemy fire would have to include both direct fire, such as rounds from pistols, rifles, and indirect fire, such as artillery, rockets and mortars.[203] As with mental retardation, the burden of proof would lie with the party purporting to be part of this proposed class. Evidence may be drawn from military records, eyewitness and expert testimony. These documents can all be relied on by the military member or veteran who would have to establish that he or she was exposed to enemy fire or took part in firing upon the enemy which caused them to develop PTSD.[204]

---

[202] *Id.*

[203] *Id.*

[204] *Id.* at 2989.

Another requirement would be that the veteran was suffering from Post-Traumatic Stress Disorder at the time of his or her offense. The defense would have the burden of proving that the veteran suffered from PTSD at the time he or she committed the crime. In addition, any prior diagnoses of PTSD will have to be based upon a medical evaluation utilizing the DSM-IV criteria as outlined.[205]

Lastly, for a diagnosis of PTSD to be service related, some form of military service has to be the primary cause of the injury in the opinion of the testifying medical expert.[206] This determination is not hard to establish as the U.S. Department of Veterans Affairs has a current disability rating process at medical treatment facilities which provides an existing method that may easily be adopted by the Courts.[207]

---

[205] U.S. DEP'T OF VETERANS AFFAIRS, VA HEALTH CARE ELIGIBILITY & ENROLLMENT, available at http://www.va.gov/healtheligibilty/Library/Glossary/#s, (last visited Aug. 3, 2012).

[206] *Id.*

[207] *Id*

CHAPTER 13

SOCIETY AND CONTEMPORARY VALUES

Objective indicia of society's morals and contemporary values definitely support the acceptance of a categorical exclusion from the death penalty for military members and combat veterans who suffer from service related PTSD and commit capital crimes.[208] As of today, there are three state legislatures which include California, Minnesota and Connecticut and four large cities which include Anchorage, Alaska; Tulsa, Oklahoma; Edwardsville, Illinois; and Buffalo, New York, which have policies which deal with the treatment of military members and veterans in a different manner when they are convicted of crimes.[209] These policies deal with these individuals through diversion programs and veterans' courts which recognize the veterans' diminished culpability in comparison to the

---

[208] Giardino, *supra* note 130, at 2989.

[209] Giardino, *supra* note 130, at 2990.

average offender.[210] These policies are very important as they carry a "special force in light of the general popularity of anticrime legislation."[211]

Public opinion and legislative policies in support of military members and veterans who suffer from PTSD also depict objective evidence of a national consensus that supports recognizing these individuals as a distinct and unique group worthy of special treatment by the government and under the law.[212]

There is evidence of a growing tide of support by the public from hundreds of yellow ribbons on vehicles, light poles, mailboxes to politicians making broad campaign promises to take care of veterans who have served their country in a time of need. It appears that popular sentiment supports those individuals who have served in Iraq and Afghanistan

---

[210] *Id.*

[211] *Id.*

[212] Shin, *supra* note 133, at 494-96, 502-04.

and favors helping them instead of sentencing them to death.[213]

The views of professional organizations also serve as objective evidence in support of a categorical exclusion for military members and veterans who suffer from combat related PTSD at the time of their offense.[214] In August 2008, the American Bar Association (ABA) supported such an exclusion to combat veterans.[215] Shortly thereafter, the American Psychiatric Association, the American Psychological Association and the National Alliance of the Mentally Ill all endorsed the ABA support.

This type of support further solidifies that there is a national consensus behind treating military members and veterans who suffer from service-related PTSD differently

---

[213] Matthew J. Friedman, Editorial, *Acknowledging the Psychiatric Cost of War,* 351 NEW ENG. J. MED. 75-76 (2004).

[214] Atkins, 536 U.S. at 316; Giardino, supra note 130, at 2991; Shin, supra note 133, at 479.

[215] American Bar Association Task Force on Mental Disability and the Death Penalty, Recommendation and Report on the Death Penalty and Persons with Mental Disabilities, 30 MENTAL & PHYSICAL DISABILITY L. REP. 668 (2006).

under the law and acknowledges that "they too have a

diminished culpability relative to the average offender."[216]

---

[216] Id.

CHAPTER **14**

THE U.S. SUPREME COURT

With indications that there may be national support for a categorical exclusion for these individuals, it is incumbent upon the United States Supreme Court to apply its own independent judgment to determine "whether the death penalty is a disproportionate punishment for [a class of offenders]."[217] This should lead the Court to the same conclusions that are very similar to those found within Atkins v. Virginia.[218]

In applying the Court's own judgment and taking into consideration the subjective factors defined within this study, the Court would surely find that the goals of the death penalty would best be served by not executing a military member or veterans who suffers from combat

---

[217] *Roper v. Simmons*, 543 U.S. 551, 564 (2005).

[218] *Atkins v. Virginia*, 536 U.S. 304, 318-21 (2002).

related PTSD on many of the same grounds as discussed regarding the mentally retarded in Atkins.[219] The retributive purposes of the death penalty are not served by executing any individual who falls within this proposed class of offenders due to the diminished culpability of one suffering from PTSD and surely does not warrant the death penalty "[if]f the culpability of the average murderer is insufficient to justify the most extreme sanction available to the State."[220] The deterrent goals of the death penalty are not furthered by executing the proposed category of military members or veterans because as a result of the judgment-impaired effects of PTSD at the time of the offense, it would be "less likely that they [could] process the information of the possibility of execution as a penalty sand, as a result,

---

[219] *Id.*

[220] *Atkins*, 536 U.S. at 319.

control the conduct based upon that information."[221]

By conducting the same type of analysis as it did in Atkins, the Court would find that PTSD symptoms drastically affect judgment so as to render combat veterans suffering from those conditions similar to, if not less culpable than, the mentally impaired.[222]

The symptoms offered within this study undoubtedly show that PTSD is very similar to the mental retardation category. This is proven by the significantly diminished ability of some military members and veterans to appreciate the wrongfulness of their conduct and their failure to conform to the requirements of the law.[223]

The Court should also examine the role of the governments training that military members and veterans are placed through and the role that it plays in the diminished

---

[221] *Atkins,* 536 U.S. at 320; Giardino, *supra* note 130, at 2993.

[222] Giardino, *supra* note 130, at 2993.

[223] *Id.*

culpability of combat veterans to further support a categorical exclusion. Compared to civilians who develop PTSD through an abnormally traumatic experience, a service member experiences and develops a higher degree of severe anger, increased hypervigilance, and startle responses. [224]

This can be caused by the service member's basic training experience which is designed to change the typical behavior pattern within the human response known as the "Fight" or "Flight" syndrome. An individual's instinctive response when faced with confrontation or danger is to run or "Flight." This is the basic human response which the brain transmits to the body which serves no purpose in a war zone.

[224] The author acknowledges this statement is self-purported by personal experiences and vast military training. The author served sixteen years on active duty with the United States military in the Department of the Air Force. The positions and opinions stated herein are those of the author alone and do not represent the views of the U.S. Government, the Department of Defense, the Department of the Air Force or any other governmental agency.

Military members are trained to stay in the "Fight."[225] From the moment a service member arrives at basic training, the "recruit" is constantly berated with verbal insults and demoralizing feats of both mental and physical tasks. Subsequent training involves drills which range from very basic maneuvers such as standing at attention and at ease to basic marching in a formation.[226] A military member is taught this until they instinctively perform these movements without thought. At this point, their actions have been changed from voluntary to involuntary and they intuitively perform moves when ordered by their superior.[227] Additional training could place some of these service members into stress related exercises that may range from basic rifle marksmanship which allows the recruit to shoot

---

[225] *Id.*

[226] *Id.*

[227] *Id.*

at a man-shaped target, to the infamous Survive, Evade, Resist, Escape (SERE) training which educates military members such as aviators, Special Forces or rescue operators who are at a high risk of capture.[228] This training places the service member in situations which allow them to develop the skillsets necessary to survive and evade capture or, if captured, to resist interrogation or exploitation and plan their escape.[229] The type of training also includes classroom phases, field phases and a resistance training laboratory which simulates the environment of a prisoner-of-war compound.[230]

With this insight, the Court should find it unconscionable for the government to sentence any combat solider or veteran to death for their criminal actions that would have more than likely not occurred had it been for their service

---

[228] *Id.*

[229] *Id.*

[230] *Id.*

and government-sponsored training. The combination of impaired judgment and the military training drastically interferes with the ability of the service member or veteran to appreciate the wrongfulness of the act of killing and to conform their conduct to the requirements of the law.[231]

---

[231] Giardino, *supra* note 130, at 2995.

CHAPTER **15**

CONCLUSION

From the cases presented, it seems evident that the best way to communicate to the courts that PTSD and the death penalty is a vital concern among veterans, is to take responsibility as a country for these service members suffering and for their resulting criminal actions. This can be accomplished from presenting a comprehensive legal defense, which centers combat related PTSD as a diminished capacity, to establishing a categorical exclusion as discussed within this study. It has to be extremely clear that this type of defense or category can only be utilized by defendants who have been charged with intentional first-degree murder as opposed to homicide charges where specific intent is not an element of proof. Veterans who face the death penalty should be excluded from the death penalty as this sentence is cruel and usual.

It is our responsibility as a nation to provide mental health services to service members and veterans who have put their lives and families on the line for our country and to ensure that when these mental health services fail, we do not hold our veterans accountable for the wrongs that they commit as a result of mental damage that they incurred on our behalf.[232] To this end, a greater focus on PTSD at trial to humanize and explain the crimes of veterans is necessary. All legal professionals to include the defense, prosecutors, juries and the judges should familiarize themselves with the legal defenses based on PTSD so that they can effectively engage with these defenses at trial in a way that respects the lives and sacrifices of our combat service members and veterans.[233]

Since the existence of service-related Post-Traumatic Stress Disorder in combat veterans reduces the personal culpability, these individuals should not be regarded as

---

[232] *Id.*

[233] Loomer-Johnson, *supra* note 99, at 29.

"among the worst offenders" and should not be subjected to the death penalty.[234] Because the characteristics of PTSD are so closely related to those of mental retardation, this merits a categorical exclusion from the death penalty. This exclusion for service members and combat veterans suffering from PTSD at the time of the offense must be created by legislatures or the courts to ensure that only the worst offenders receive the ultimate punishment.[235]

[234] Giardino, *supra* note 130, at 2995.

[235] *Id.*